To John & Rose Ellen Sofer

From Luke and Rosalie McBride
Sofer

WINES FROM
A SMALL GARDEN

WINES FROM A SMALL GARDEN

planting to bottling

James Page-Roberts

ABBEVILLE PRESS   PUBLISHERS
NEW YORK   LONDON   PARIS

First published in the United States of America in 1995
by Abbeville Press

First published in Great Britain in 1995 by The Herbert Press
Ltd, 46 Northchurch Road, London N1 4EJ
Copyright © 1995 by James Page-Roberts

House editor Brenda Herbert
Designed by Pauline Harrison

Printed in Hong Kong / China. The text of this book
was set in Bembo. First edition.

10 9 8 7 6 5 4 3 2

ISBN 0-7892-0076-7

CONTENTS

VINES & WINES
IN A SMALL GARDEN

INTRODUCTION

This book is about the many pleasures and benefits to be had from growing a vine or two in a small garden where the weather is not too extreme. Except for greenhouse grapes destined for the table, we have, for some reason, mostly left the growing of grapes outdoors to the professionals in winemaking nations. There is no reason for this at all. Most vines will thrive in most climates if planted sensibly, surviving the heat of the North African desert fringes and the winter iciness of North America.

There is great satisfaction to be had from planting, training and pruning your vine, and from the pleasures of resting in the shade beneath a canopy of leaves and grapes, of enjoying the colour of summer and autumn foliage, of using the leaves in the kitchen, of eating the fruit, of drinking freshly-pressed juice, of vinification, of making wonderful vinegar and, finally, of drinking wine that will be purer than any available for sale in the shops – and almost all of this for free. ·

How could any sensible gardener resist growing vines when no patch of soil is too small to accommodate at least one?

A VERY SHORT HISTORY OF WINE

Prehistoric people found grapes growing on wild vines, ate the fruit and squashed the grapes in their hands or under foot to make juice. When they tried to keep this juice for a day or two in their simple clay pots, they noticed that it had begun to bubble and take on a different character. (They did not know then that yeasts from grape skins were at work turning sugar into alcohol.) The fermented result was terrific and led to many a splendid and probably procreative party. Wine had appeared on the global scene.

However, it quickly became obvious that with an abundance of flies and microbes at large, this newly made and exciting beverage soon turned sour. There was no way to preserve it, so it was drunk right away.

Also at that time, it was discovered that a donkey (or more likely a goat) had chewed up a straggling vine in the winter, leaving nothing in the ground but an unsightly stump. Then, in summer, to general delight, from the gnarled wood grew a fine vine, producing a large crop of excellent quality grapes. So the art of pruning was established.

We now take a great leap forward in time to when the Phoenician businessmen plied their trade across the seas of the then known world. Wine was one of their cargoes, and it was transported in amphorae, stacked in racks aboard ship. Now wine in these containers quite naturally attracted flies and germs and soon went off; so to keep the insects away, a layer of olive oil was floated on top. This also preserved the wine both by keeping the insects and bacteria at bay and by preventing oxygen in the air from oxidizing the wine (which, like the action of yeasts, was something else that was to be discovered very much later).

This was all fine until a storm blew up at sea. The wine spilled, which may have done a lot to help preserve the ship's timbers and improve the atmosphere, but did nothing for business. So a plug had to be found, and it took the form of pinewood discs, which were bedded into the necks of amphorae with a clay and resin mixture. Discs of cork may also have been used with a similar bonding compound.

The resinous wood and sealing mixture flavoured the wine as they came in contact in rolling seas. The Phoenicians and Greeks came to believe that resin preserved the wine. Anyhow, a taste was acquired for it, which has survived until this day, in the form of Retsina wine which is stored in barrels with lumps of resin.

Ahead we go again, this time to ancient Rome, its empire and army. To keep the legionaries happy and healthy, each was given a daily ration of a litre of wine. But as the armies advanced over Europe, lines of supply were stretched to the limit. So the wily Romans planted vines wherever they went to reduce the burden on these lines of supply. The wines they found and developed in Worms, for instance, became so good over the centuries that in the eighteenth century, an Englishman called Maximilian Mission wrote that the monks there thought the wines were as delicious and as sweet as milk from the Holy Virgin (hence today's Liebfrau(en)milch). What a legacy!

When the Romans reached England, their lines of supply and communication had become even longer and more perilous. So, again, vines were introduced, and for the first time. The variety planted to produce the daily ration may have been Wrotham Pinot (on test in my London garden at present). Wine-growing in the UK since then has been a spasmodic business and generally on a small scale. In the late 1950s there was a resurgence of interest in Britain under the guidance of R. Barrington Brock. There are now some large commercial vineyards in operation; and we can but wish the owners good luck. But if I were to invest in vineyards on a commercial scale, I would go elsewhere. Vines and wines in the garden for fun and decoration is quite a different matter.

Since the fall of the Roman Empire, through times of

prosperity, plague, wars and famine, winemaking skills have progressed, until it has now become a high-tech industry in Europe, Asia, Africa, the Antipodes and the Americas. Wine is also made in China, India, Japan, Holland, Denmark, Sweden and elsewhere. Suitable microclimates can be found in the most unlikely places. Vines seem to have no bounds.

We have skipped lightly through history until arriving at this very instant, where, if you now read on and follow my simple instructions, you will plant vines like the Romans, squish grapes like the ancients, ferment the juice in the same way as generations of winemakers everywhere, cork the bottles rather like the Phoenicians, prune your vines a bit like the donkey, and drink the wine in the same joyous spirit that every civilized person has done since time immemorial.

WHY POISON OURSELVES?

Although I once almost ruined a vintage when too much sulphur spray entered the winery on grapeskins, it was not until I was visiting a vineyard in the Cahors region of France and saw grapes harvested with a thick coating of blue copper (used, with sulphur, almost universally as spray or dust throughout the growing season by professional winemakers to combat mildew and rot) that I came to the conclusion that spray, of any kind, should be avoided if humanly possible. But with grapes this presents difficulties.

Most of the finest quality vines are the pure and cross-bred European varieties (*Vitis vinifera*). These are disease-prone and need prophylactic spray. They would also be subject to the dreaded phylloxera louse if grown on their own roots, so they have to be grafted on to phylloxera-resistant American rootstocks. Disease-resistant vines, not needing spray, are mostly hybrids with origins that are part, or all, from the North American continent. So to avoid the use of prophylactic or disease-killing spray preparations, it will be to this latter category of vines that we turn our attention.

Spraying on the soil to suppress weeds or kill grass around your vines should also be avoided. I am unconvinced that vines do not ingest these chemicals. But in a small plot, the elimination of grass and weeds is a comparatively simple task, best done with hoe, fork or trowel.

Sprays, even when used with care on vines, can also touch neighbouring plants, and sometimes neighbours and their plants, not to mention yourself. So it is sensible to avoid spraying, for the health of the soil, the vine, and the human race.

OUTDOOR VINE VARIETIES AND LOCATIONS

The following descriptions have been gleaned first-hand over a period of twenty-five years of growing vines in two different vineyards, and now in a small London garden, where, after the elimination of some unworthy examples, fifteen selected varieties have been on test, some of which have still to reach maturity. This selection has been reached by looking originally for vines not subject to disease and then putting to the test the vines with possibilities. The search has become more intensive since I became aware that the ingestion of chemicals used in vineyard management and winemaking might be harmful to the health and cause headaches.

When I first became interested in eliminating chemically noxious sprays, I wrote in the then published garden and wine magazines asking readers to let me know if they were growing any satisfactory grapevines free of disease, mildew and rot. From the many replies I received, the most mentioned variety was the Strawberry Grape. Many readers had successful vines which they described but were unable to name. Some must have been Brant. One correspondent even grew Müller-Thurgau free of disease in Essex. He was extremely lucky. For me it has been a troublesome vine in past years, needing a regular spray regime to combat rot and mildew (the former coating the fruit with a grey mould and the latter being Powdery or Downy Mildew that attacks leaves and destroys fruit).

The vines I have grown have started their lives as cuttings (sometimes rooted, sometimes not) and in containers bought from garden centres. The advantage of starting with cuttings (see WINTER PRUNING, page 92) is that they are either cheap or free. They must be planted in the dormant winter months. Container-grown vines, on the other hand, may be planted at any time of the year and will produce grapes in a shorter time; but they will be more expensive. Do not expect fruit for three years.

Any gardener who has planted a tree dug directly from a nursery's land, and a tree grown in a container, will have noticed, if having to move them when established, that the nursery-grown tree will have settled into the soil far more happily than its container-grown companion – however well the roots of the latter were teased out at planting time. The choice is yours. Incidentally, never be afraid to chop off side roots after the vine has become established, nor, for that matter, to dig up and destroy an unsatisfactory vine however near it is to a successful one. And you can rototill right up to an established vine without hurting it. In fact, by cutting off surface roots you will be root pruning, and this will strengthen the vine. Do not be afraid to move a vine if it

An arbour of vines in a small town garden approx. 9×3m (30×10 ft)

is in the wrong place. I have transferred four-year-old vines from one position to another with no apparent harm done.

Some of the varieties of vine mentioned here may not be acceptable for commercial use in mainland Europe. But we are not interested in that, though Seyval Blanc, Cascade, Siegerrebe, Wrotham Pinot and Triomphe d'Alsace are all authorized for use in English vineyards.

Times of bud-burst, flowering, fruiting and harvest, when stated in the following descriptions, are for southern England or similar temperate climates at, or near, sea level, when the vine is grown in a sheltered position and with access to the sun. These times of the year will be later if the vines are grown farther north, at altitude or in harsher conditions. Vines thrive outside, and wine is made from their grapes, even as far north as, for example, Stirling in Scotland if planted in a sheltered and sunny position. Many are hardy in north USA and Canada. Successful ripening of fruit will depend on the season. Altitude, exposure to cold winds and a sunless site will always mean later growth and harvest. Frost may damage a vine where the winter weather is really extreme. But even in such conditions it is worth trying to grow a vine and protecting it with some insulating material. Vines are very hardy; and even a frost or two on ripening grapes will do no harm (grapes for the famous German Eiswein are harvested in their solid, frozen state). Vines do not particularly like humid, tropical conditions but thrive in the very hot and dry climate of North Africa and in the irrigated deserts of Spain. They even thrive, at altitude, on the equator in Kenya, where goats' blood is used as fertilizer, though this attracts snakes. They will stand the cold of upper New York State and grow throughout much of Europe through Holland, Denmark and even in secluded corners of Sweden. They will grow at altitude above tropical humidity and in many an untoward location when the site has been judiciously chosen. (Read more about soil and site on pages 38–42.)

Always with disease resistance in mind, let us start with the recommended white grape. There is only one. I wish there were more, but I have not found any, unless the white version of the Strawberry Grape (see later) is included.

SEYVAL BLANC (once Seyve Villard 5276), a cross between European and North American varieties, is one of the best for generosity of fruit, vigour and disease resistance. This vine starts to grow and form flower heads in April (a little later than some vines). There may be uneven growth from the spurs (see WINTER PRUNING, page 93). Flowers open and are self-pollinated in early June. The leaves are healthy (though I did once see a slight sign

A fruiting vine trained along a wall provides a division between gardens

of mildew on an example grown on a wall in Hampshire). No spray will be necessary, but the beautiful green fruit can split if the vine is over-watered (by man or nature).

The grapes will be ready to harvest in late September. Their sugar content is on the low side, but this will increase with later harvesting. In a wet autumn, however, split grapes may become mouldy, thus precipitating harvest time to prevent rot from tainting the wine.

The wine quality is never the greatest, being somewhat acidic and short of flavour, but when fermented in the skins (see WINEMAKING, page 74) more taste will be imparted to the wine. Nevertheless, there have been commercial winemakers who have made prize-winning wine from this variety.

Seyval Blanc grapes will blend well when vinified with those of any of the black grapes recommended below, bulking up the volume, adding acidity and forming a rosé-coloured wine. The proportions of your blends will depend on the ripe grapes available at the time. This will vary from season to season, and is one of those matters of chance that make home wine production such a delight.

SUMMARY: Despite the occasional seasonal lapse when the grapes split and then rot, I consider Seyval Blanc to be the best white grape for cultivation in a small garden.

THE STRAWBERRY GRAPE (of North American origin) can be white, black or white turning pink, so let us deal with it here. This healthy, popular and productive vine was a favourite for grapes and wine with the English aristocracy in the eighteenth century. It was once grown extensively in the Dijon region of France, and, contrary to EU regulations, is still grown in its black form in the Veneto region of Italy. As I mentioned earlier, it was the most popular vine with the correspondents who replied to my letter in gardening and wine magazines requesting information on disease-free vines.

From a peeling bark, the buds are slow to burst forth in spring. But when they do, they are tight, pink and green, and very attractive. Having appeared, they open quickly to show leaf and then small green flower buds, later to open and self-pollinate from mid to late June. These soon become well formed bunches of maturing grapes. The fruit is large when compared with other hybrid varieties. Growing tips are very pale.

The thick, healthy leaves, with felty undersides, are not the best for stuffing. When the grapes are ripening, the leaves begin to turn mottled yellows with green veins.

The fruit of the Strawberry Grape turns strawberry colour when almost ripe (though some clones are green or black). At this time (late September to early October), they may be

harvested for the table when tested and found pleasant. The juice will have a distinctive 'American foxy' taste, not dissimilar to that of the popular Concord grape (with origins in Concord, Massachusetts) from which America's Welch's Grape Juice is made. Those who find the taste to be delicious – and in my experience they are in the majority – might use the grapes for winemaking. But they are really more suitable for the table, for flavouring fruit salads and for juice.

Among other, better known American hybrid vines in the same category as the Strawberry Grape are the black Catawba, considered by the French authority Pierre Galet to be sensitive to mildew and the dreaded phylloxera louse; white Noah, hardy and productive; and black Othello, subject to phylloxera and disliking too much lime in the soil, but very fertile, frost-resistant and very foxy.

If juice from the Strawberry Grape fruit (or its similar tasting, foxy fellows) is added to the fermentation of others, its flavour will dominate the blend, being, perhaps, to your taste.

SUMMARY: This is a fine, decorative, extremely healthy and vigorous vine, but try the grapes first if you aim to grow the vine for more than garden decoration.

Now we come to the black grape varieties which, surprisingly, do extremely well in temperate conditions. As some have red juice (unusual in black grapes), the resultant wine is of a most wonderful, deep ruby colour.

TRIOMPHE D'ALSACE is a very strong grower. So to cover a large area, this vine must be a top choice. It is also free of mildew and rot. The heavy crop of black grapes form in dense bunches resembling clusters of large blackcurrants, oblong in shape. The juice is initially pink, becoming darker red when the grapes have ripened. This is an advantage, giving your wine a splendid colour. It is what the French call a 'teinturier' – adding to a red wine extra depth of colour (blackcurrant and elderfruit juice have also been known to be used for this purpose). If turned into juice (without the colour transfer from skins to juice that comes with fermentation) a reasonably coloured product will result. The juice can attain as much as 17–20 per cent sugar when the grapes have ripened in mid September.

The opening buds, pale green and pink to red in colour, burst forth in early April to reveal green leaves with pink edges. The vestigial bunches soon flower and self-pollinate to become part of a large crop of black grapes.

*Inspecting Triomphe
d'Alsace grapes*

Occasionally, in late summer, there is a sign of *Botrytis* (see NOBLE ROT, page 66). This only occurs in small areas of the vine. The affected grapes are a benefit to the vinification. Triomphe d'Alsace leaves are excellent for kitchen use until late summer (see STUFFED VINE LEAVES, page 118). In the autumn they turn a beautiful lemon yellow colour and 'light up' the garden.

SUMMARY: This is my most recommended vine for small-garden cultivation. As an all-rounder for growth, health, crop, edible leaves and autumn colour it is a winner. The wine made from its grapes is robust and deeply coloured.

CASCADE (once Seibel 13053) is a strong and healthy vine producing a good crop of black grapes in open bunches that make a wine somewhat resembling Beaujolais Nouveau. The vine is winter hardy in New York State. I have given away many cuttings, and in every case the recipients have been delighted. As with the other varieties recommended here, no spraying is needed.

The first pink leaves burst forth from tight, pointed buds in early to mid April. Flowering and self-pollination take place in the first part of June.

Cascade makes a fine and decorative cover for an arbour or arch with its cascading bunches of grapes, ripening from early to mid September. The juice is coloured. The red-stemmed, indented, sometimes blotchy leaves dry out in late September.

Although excellent for small gardens, Cascade is less suitable for larger-scale wine production because in each bunch of ripe grapes are some that never progress beyond the green stage. This does not matter for the small-scale producer of wine when the vinifier will hand strip the ripe fruit from every bunch.

SUMMARY: Cascade is, in most respects, a first class black grape for a small garden.

RUSSIAN GAGARIN (named after the first astronaut) is a fairly recent addition to my collection of vines. This strong, healthy and vigorous vine has already shown great potential. An interesting feature is its tendency to grow horizontally (and this makes it excellent for an arbour or pergola). If left to form a spreading bush, it will root itself where the canes touch the ground.

A late April or early May burst of long, yellow ochre leaf buds lead to the formation of flower buds and red-ribbed leaves on long red stems. Flowering takes place in early June. The open

*Fruit of the Strawberry
Grape and Cascade*

bunches of fruit will become bronze/blue before ripening to become black grapes with red juice. I have, until now, blended its juice with that of Triomphe d'Alsace and Cascade for September vinification (I have mentioned earlier the charm of chance blends. Record them – see KEEPING A RECORD, page 109).

My cousin, a retired professor of chemistry, has, for many years, had a vine growing untrained on the bank of a stream. He finds it to be bountiful, disease-free and bird-resistant. He swears by Russian Gagarin, and so may I.

SUMMARY: A lovely vine and a great prospect.

OTHER POSSIBLE VARIETIES

BRANT, a vine of Canadian origin, is more of a decorative vine than one for wine. The low sugar content of its black grapes make it suitable only for juice and blending.

After bud burst in early April, the pale yellow-green leaves hold tightly together before opening. Then they change colour to become an attractive pattern of green and reddish-copper.

So Brant must be considered primarily as a vine for garden decoration. Grown with other varieties in an arbour, it adds colourful zest to the overall green canopy, especially in the autumn. Its fruit will ripen later than others recommended here. If not quite a winner, Brant makes an excellent companion vine. It is disease-free and a strong grower.

SIEGERREBE is another on my short list of possible vines for a small garden. Slower to grow than some of the others, and with uneven growth from spurs, its handsome, early ripening, bricky red fruit is sweet and delicious – in a muscaty, perfumed kind of way.

Its pinky buds and yellow-green unfurling leaves of early to mid April mature to become somewhat bumpy. The growing tips are whitish.

Siegerrebe's very sweet grapes are good for eating, juice and blending. But there is a big snag: in mid to late August, wasps are attracted to the grapes as much as humans, and keeping those stinging pests at bay is an almost impossible task. As soon as the grapes ripen, they are sucked dry, leaving shrivelled and unsightly stems on the vine. But in some years and in some districts and conditions, you may be successful and reap a fine harvest of its flavoursome fruit. *Botrytis* can also cause early damage to bunches.

To grow Siegerrebe on a wall (where it will do best) is possibly a risk worth taking if you enjoy a contest and have space for more suitable varieties of vine. But I do not recommend it wholeheartedly.

BACO No.1 is a black grape of French origin. The strongest grower of those recommended here, it fruits well but can easily get out of hand. To ramble and cover an unsightly building, it is ideal. The large leaves turn colour and dry out unevenly in the autumn. Use its juice for blending.

The number of vines grown in temperate conditions, mostly for vineyards, is myriad – among the most popular being the whites Müller-Thurgau, Seyval Blanc, Reichensteiner, Schönburger, Hüxelrebe, Bacchus, Gewürztraminer, Ortega, Madeleine Angevine, Chardonnay, Riesling and Kerner. The reds, though far less popular, and generally cultivated under experimental conditions and to give colour for rosé wine, are Pinot Noir (the most popular), Gamay, Triomphe d'Alsace, Cascade, Zweigeltrebe and Léon Millot. Over the years I have counted more than eighty under cultivation or recommended for commercial use. Many have their adherents. Most need spraying, some are troublesome, others plain unsuitable. But as I have mentioned (I hope forcefully), in whatever country you happen to be, avoid any variety subject to rot or mildew that needs spraying, as even when in proximity to a disease-resistant vine, the noxious spores from an unhealthy vine can, and will, contaminate its healthy neighbours.

A very successful black French hybrid vine, frowned upon officially as not being of noble stock, is Chambourcin. Those I have seen growing in the UK (and I am now growing one myself) have looked very promising. A black grape from France with a good reputation is Plantet. Villard Noir is another.

In the USA, beside the ubiquitous east coast Concord, already mentioned as a prime prospect for juice if not wine, the black Rubired is a distinct possibility for warmer areas. For the cooler parts, try Maréchal Foch. Popular whites in the USA are Niagara (foxy) and Cayuga.

I have witnessed many vines furnished with edible grapes growing happily on decorative and shady arbours in hot countries where vines thrive. There may be some that are disease-free, but those I have seen, like their vineyard neighbours, have been sprayed with copper, and probably sulphur, as protection from disease. The vines we are dealing with here are disease-resistant varieties for decoration and wine, especially chosen for more temperate climes.

For an unheated greenhouse vine in cool climates I recommend the Black Hamburgh as the best all round for cropping, grape size and flavour. For a winter heated greenhouse, a vine needing almost professional care and attention is the white Muscat of Alexandria. It is the vine grown in the greenhouses of great estates where gardeners abound and money is not a consideration.

ACQUIRING YOUR VINES

Where do you find your vines? As in other forms of gardening, the first place to look and enquire is in your locality. Ask for advice at every turn. It will be readily given. You do not need to accept any of it, but it will teach you a lot. Garden centres, nurserymen (and women), suppliers of vines, will all help, sell to you and give advice. In your travels you may have seen a vine growing healthily and producing a good crop of grapes. The owner of it will almost certainly give you a cutting in the dormant season or allow you to take one (see TAKING CUTTINGS, page 104). Try more than one variety. Do not be afraid to destroy any that fail in some respect (I do it often) and replace with those more suitable. And when you do have established vines in your garden, and are enjoying the immense pleasure they have to offer, I need hardly suggest that you, in turn, are generous with cuttings and advice. As I have mentioned elsewhere, rooted cuttings make fine presents.

SOIL, SITE, POSITION, SPACING AND PLANTING

About the only type of soil disliked by vines is when it is soggy and poorly drained. Almost any other earth will be acceptable, whether it is acid or alkaline, heavy or light.

To plant a vine in clay soil, dig a hole larger than the expanse of your new vine's

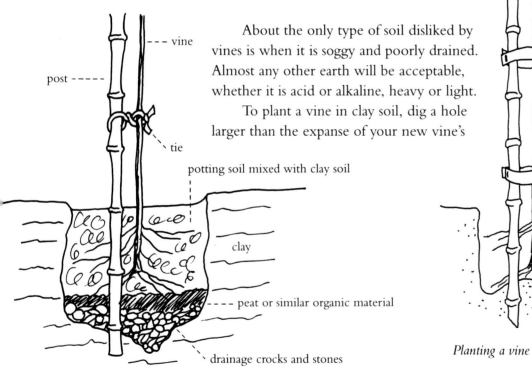

How to plant in heavy clay soil

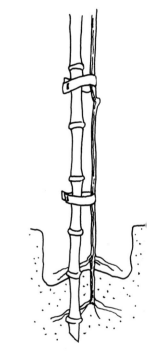

Planting a vine

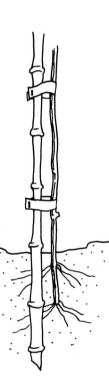

roots. Make it as deep as possible, without, of course, overdoing it by disturbing heavy sub-soil. Push in a bamboo cane on which to tie the planted vine later. In the bottom of the hole scatter shards from broken clay pots and, if they are plentiful, stones from the garden. On this put a good layer of moistened peat, purchased planting medium or well-rotted garden compost. Hold the vine close to the bamboo and, keeping to the depth at which the vine had been previously planted, pack in a mixture of the original clay soil mixed with any of a lighter composition, such as loam, compost and grit. Make sure that the roots of the vine radiate on a horizontal plane. There may be two layers of roots. Cover the lower one first and then the upper. Press down the earth, but do not stamp on it. Tie the vine to the bamboo and give the soil around a good soaking with water. Press down on the soil more firmly with the heel of your boot when the earth has dried out. Do this again after frosts have thawed. The vine will reward you for this initial kindness.

When planting a vine in almost any other kind of soil, proceed as above but without the added drainage and extra loam. Plant a rooted cutting or container-grown vine to the same depth as it was previously. But when planting a container-grown vine, tease out as many roots as possible that, due to the space restriction of its pot, will have formed a tight mat of rootlets.

Vines generally prefer a well-drained site on a gentle south-facing slope (north-facing in the southern hemisphere) to attract the warmth of the sun. But this is not essential; many successful vineyards are grown on other sites, and a single vine or two will grow wherever they are judiciously placed. On a windy, open site, it is beneficial to grow a few deciduous windbreak trees to break the force of winter gales or winds that might break off canes or damage grapes or other fruit in the garden. A southerly facing house wall (in the northern hemisphere) is always a good position for a vine, especially where the local climate is a cool one. Vines do not like to be planted in a frost pocket (a dip in the ground or valley where frost gathers in the springtime and is slow to clear). Late frosts in such areas can harm vine flowers.

If several varieties of vine are to be grown over an arbour or archway, and possibly allowed to continue on further around a garden after the framework has been covered, they may be planted quite close to each other, say 45cm (18 ins) or less. On the other hand, one example of a vigorous vine will, if trained properly, cover a large area.

Try not to overlap and thus crowd vines. They like a free flow of air and plenty of sunlight in summertime. But do cross the main stems over each other as much as wanted when the buds are rubbed out to allow the vine(s) to reach the place where you

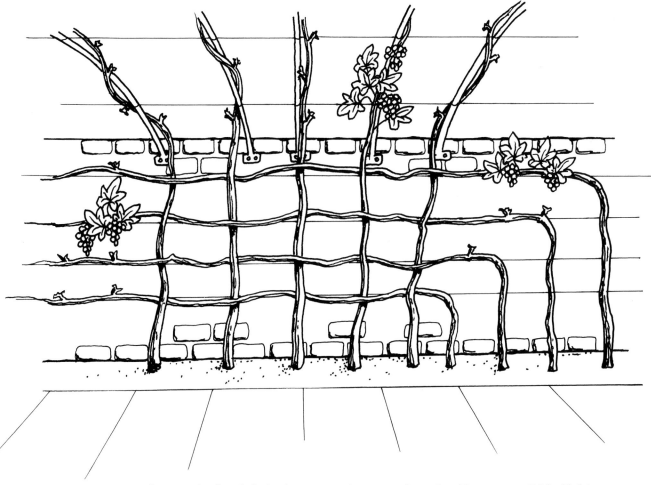

want them to leaf and fruit. (I am creating a meshwork of inter-woven vine stocks where disbudded, horizontally-trained vine sections mesh with disbudded verticals.)

Disbudded interwoven vines on a wall

Other plants lying close to vines will be in competition for water and nourishment. If this is the case, you must be more generous with water and fertilizer (see WATERING, page 60).

Nothing in gardening is 'instant'. Consideration and patience is always needed. You may want your vine to flower and fruit immediately. It won't. From a rooted cutting allow three years before flowers and fruit come to anything. An unrooted cutting will take longer. But when established, a vigorous vine will grow about 3 metres (10 ft) or more each year if not checked. To encourage the vine to form a framework or reach a destination, discourage fruiting initially by pinching out the flower heads and side shoots (see INITIAL TRAINING, page 49).

VINES GROWN IN POTS

Vines grow well in pots. Almost all vines, and any of those recommended, will succeed. The excellent Black Hamburgh will do well if wintered outside and brought into a greenhouse at fruiting and ripening time.

A good layer of drainage crocks placed at the bottom of an earthenware pot about 30cm (12 ins) to 38cm (15 ins) wide is essential. (You may have difficulty in moving larger pots.)

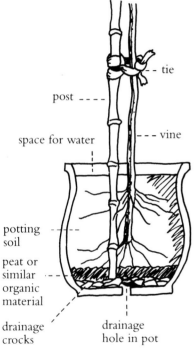

post - - - -

space for water

tie

vine

potting soil

peat or similar organic material

drainage crocks

drainage hole in pot

Vine in pot

Vines grown in pots

Tease out the roots of a previously container-grown vine, plant with a stout post and pack around it good quality compost, or a packaged commercial potting soil. Leave a good gap between soil level and pot rim to allow for watering.

Pruning pot-grown vines is best contrived by the fountain method.

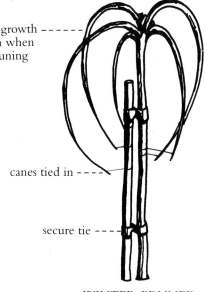

summer's new canes for next year's fruiting

summer's growth tied down when winter pruning

fruiting canes from previous summer's growth to be cut away when winter pruning

canes tied in

secure tie

support post

rub off all buds that grow from trunk

VINE IN POT WINTER PRUNED

WINTER PRUNED

SUMMER

Fountain pruning for flower beds and pots

43

Vines in decorative pots, from carved stonework on a C14 Sicilian church doorway

Vines grown in pots

Watering the vine throughout the summer is necessary, as is the regular application of a little balanced fertilizer and a pinch of trace elements (see pages 60–61). As with all plants in pots, overfeeding can be very damaging. A certain amount of soil-replacement each year is an advantage, as is potting on established vines that have been started in a smallish pot.

If the vine is wintered outside, be sure to secure the pot by partially, or totally, burying it in the ground. This has the advantage of preventing the wind from blowing it over and saving the earthenware from splitting in the frost.

A pot-grown vine will last for many years and provide good crops, though not as long as a vine grown outside, where life expectancy is forty-five years or more. Pot-grown vines must be fed and watered correctly (adequately but not too much).

VINES ON ARBOURS, ARCHES, PERGOLAS, IN BEDS AND ON WIRES

The advantages of an arbour or arch in a small garden are that it can form a decorative feature, sometimes a focal point, provide shade in the summer and a structure that you and the vine will appreciate when the grapes hang freely from below it.

44

For spectacular effect, this arbour could stretch from party wall to party wall of the garden of a terraced house, forming one or several arches with one or more vines, as illustrated on page 50. On the other hand, it might take the form of a gazebo, a summer house, or a temple housing a seat, fountain or sculpture.

An overhead pergola of wood and/or wire trelliswork supported by posts is another possible structure on which to grow vines. They can also be trained on trellis along party walls, although to trim off growth on the far side is very difficult.

You could plant a single vine to cover a large area, or several of the same variety, or a mixture of various kinds. There are no rules.

The material used for your constructions could be of softwood well treated against rot, hardwood to last longer, wire, or a structure of reinforcing rod or other metal made by a blacksmith. Any wooden material, whether softwood or hardwood, should be treated with preservative, bitumen or paint – especially the parts to be buried below ground, which should be soaked for as long as possible in a bucket or tube of preservative. Ironwork will need to be freed of rust, undercoated, top-coated twice, or covered with bitumen.

For vine training 2mm galvanized wire is adequate. When it is installed, wear rubber gloves, soak a rag in black bitumen and

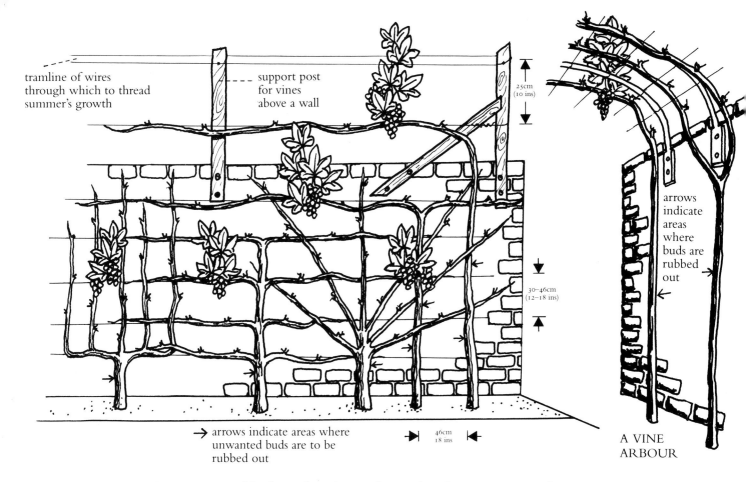

tramline of wires through which to thread summer's growth

support post for vines above a wall

25cm (10 ins)

30–46cm (12–18 ins)

arrows indicate areas where unwanted buds are to be rubbed out

46cm 18 ins

arrows indicate areas where buds are rubbed out

A VINE ARBOUR

Vines on walls and arbours (not to scale, and overcrowded for the sake of illustration)

run this along the wires and over the vine eyes to coat them. When dry, do it again. This takes the reflective shine off new wire and extends its life greatly.

Do not plant your vine(s) too close to freshly preserved wood, even when the preservative is thoroughly dry. Start your vines a short distance away, tying them to bamboo canes until they grow long enough to reach the main support.

A vine will make a fine sight in a flower or vegetable bed if
grown singly and fountain pruned (see page 96). Attached to a
strong, well-preserved post, with 1 metre (3 ft) or more above
ground level and 50cm (18 ins) below, it will form a feature that
will please you.

Vines will grow along and through wooden trelliswork,
though they may break it in time. Grown in this way they are

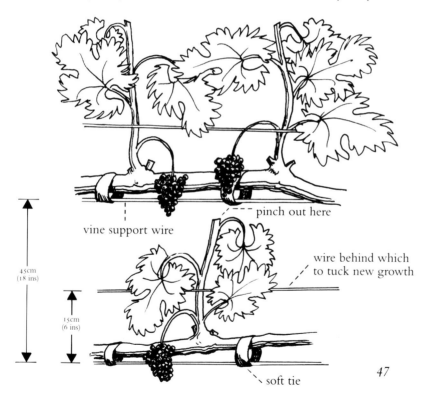

*Growth tucked behind
wire (not to scale)*

pinch out here

vine support wire

wire behind which
to tuck new growth

45cm
(18 ins)

15cm
(6 ins)

soft tie

47

difficult to prune, especially along a party wall where the new
canes will grow into a neighbour's garden. Along brick walls they
will definitely need to be wired. These wires should be attached
to the wall with vine eyes, which could be either the zinc-coated
variety, knocked into the mortar (drill a hole first before applying
the hammer), or long-hafted steel, screwed into plugged holes.
Screw eyes like the latter are the ones to use on woodwork.

Wires running parallel along walls and fences can be strung
as close as 30cm (12 ins) apart, though 45cm (18 ins) is preferable.
It is helpful to have an intermediate wire placed 15cm (6 ins)
above those holding a vine, and further away from the wall,

Vines trained around doors
and windows

behind which to tuck new season's growth; or, in the case of vines trained on wires supported by posts *above* a wall, new growth can be threaded through a tramline of wires, 25cm (10 ins) above the highest single wire (see page 46). There are many other ways to train a vine – fan, cordon, espalier – some of which are illustrated opposite and on page 53.

Several different varieties of vine grown on walls or over arches is as effective and decorative as a single kind. Brant, with its bronze/red leaves is most decorative. Triomphe d'Alsace displays fine yellow autumn foliage. The juice from crops ripening at different times, vinified separately, can be used to form blends.

INITIAL TRAINING

The buds on your cutting, rooted cutting or pot-grown vine will swell in late March and burst forth in April. There may be several buds to choose from and it will be tempting to allow them all to make shoots. But you will want to form the basic framework for your vine's future: so allow the strongest shoot to grow, with one spare in case this leader should become broken by the wind, birds, pets or yourself. The exception to this initial selection is with unrooted cuttings, when the swelling buds will be fed

Establishing a vine in a pot

Vines trained up a wall to form an arbour

Vines growing over an arbour

by residual sap in the stem, as roots will not yet have been formed. In this case, leave all the buds until roots have formed around midsummer and then select the strongest for further cosseting.

Bamboo makes excellent guides for initial growth. The stakes may be discarded later when the vine has acquired girth and strength.

Allow the main leader and any selected side branches for the framework to reach their destination over the first few years. The tip of the main growth may break off, but another bud close behind will soon take over as the leader. Side shoots will form. Except for those wanted as part of your framework, cut them off, or pinch them out above the first leaf. This will allow a spur to form for future fruiting. Keep to this vine-training technique when forming an archway, arbour, pergola, or wall display.

When the vine is established, new canes will grow (upwards) from each spur. Tuck this new growth behind wires on a wall and trim it off when it reaches the vine above. On a pergola or other structure, trim off all long and unsightly canes throughout the growing season.

Cut off, or pinch out, growing tips whenever you think it to be necessary. This will 'bush out' the vine and encourage growth in other parts. Trim with garden shears if it is easier.

cut off or pinch out side shoots from new growth after first leaf to form future spur

Treatment of first side shoots

52

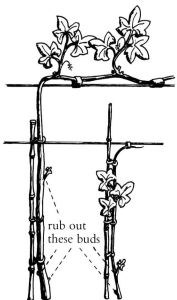

Training vines on walls: with judicious bud-rubbing and control of spurs there are absolutely no limits

For free-standing vines tied to a post, decide at what height you wish the top of your fountain to be (see page 96) and top it off just above a bud at that point.

BUD-RUBBING AND POLLINATION

All unwanted buds, which, in most varieties, will grow abundantly from the trunk (rod), must be rubbed off in early spring and thereafter as soon as they appear. If these are allowed to develop, they will form an unsightly tangle, and the vine won't like it at all. (A television interviewer to whom I was demonstrating bud-rubbing in one of my vineyards, became quite carried away with the idea of such eroticism in the garden!)

rub out
these buds

Bud-rubbing

Unwanted shoots should be rubbed off

Shoot to be rubbed off an established Triomphe d'Alsace vine

Starting an interwoven mat of disbudded vine stocks

Using this bud-rubbing technique, it is possible to plant a vine in garden soil and make it perform with leaf, flower and fruit on a high roof-terrace or balcony. Having allowed only the leader to develop in this way and reach the desired destination, just continue to rub off any buds as they appear along the trunk. In the same way, it is easy to grow the roots in a patch of garden soil and allow the vine to develop some distance away over or around a patio or hard-paved area.

On a free-standing, fountain-trained vine, all buds below the branching point should be rubbed off after the fountain height has been reached, leaving an ever-thickening, clean trunk (see pages 43 and 97).

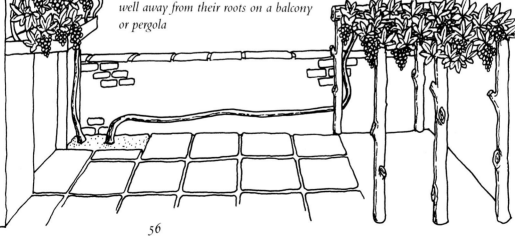

Vines can be trained to fruit and leaf well away from their roots on a balcony or pergola

56

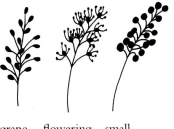

Buds growing from the previous summer season's (lighter coloured) canes are those that will form bunches of grapes in spring. Initially, the little clusters will look like miniature fruit, but they are really unopened buds that will flower in due course to self-pollinate and become grapes.

grape buds   flowering   small grapes

Do not expect to see insects pollinating your grape flowers. Vines are self-pollinating. You can help a bit by giving the vine a good shake when it is in flower. Hope for some wind, but not rain or frost, at this critical time of the year.

TYING

As growth appears and new wood becomes liable to damage by the wind, animals or you, tie it to your arch, arbour, wire or post. The quickest and easiest method for this is to use a mechanical tier, such as a Max Tapener,

A tying machine

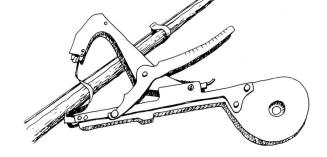

Trimming out late summer growth to allow the sunlight in to ripen the grapes

Trimming away excess growth in late summer

Inspecting the ripening crop – from left to right, Baco No.1, Seyval Blanc, the Strawberry Grape and Cascade. In the background, the foliage of Baco No.1 is just beginning to turn colour

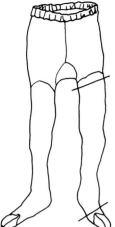

where to cut ties
from old tights

Tying

but to buy one is an expense probably not justified for small garden use. Alternatively, use any soft garden tie of your choice, such as raffia or twine. Later, when the vine has formed a thick trunk, fruit tree ties are ideal. Strips of bicycle inner tube make excellent ties but will perish in time and need to be replaced. Sections from the legs of nylon tights make soft, strong ties if not in too poor a state when discarded. They are free, if a little unsightly. Release ties and replace them when they start to bite into the bark.

WATERING AND THE USE OF FERTILIZER

In a small garden, protected by walls and/or paling, it is advisable to water your vines. Whatever the site or position, always water a vine during its first year in the ground, and for its second if the season is a dry one. Thereafter, water seldom but thoroughly during dry spells, soaking the ground to a considerable depth, otherwise root growth will form too near the soil surface and the vine will suffer in the heat. Infrequent but generous watering encourages the vine to send its roots deep in search of moisture. It will then be able to survive the driest of summers.

Especially water a vine growing next to a house or boundary wall where the soil is always driest.

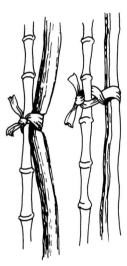

Tight ties can strangle a vine

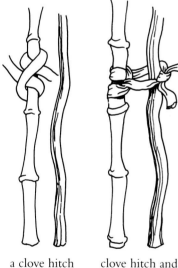

a clove hitch   clove hitch and
                     square knot

60

It is advisable to apply regularly a little general balanced fertilizer (a purchased brand such as NPK 14–14–14 or an organic alternative) to vines growing in cramped quarters and where neighbouring plants demand nutrients. It is also worth applying a mixture of trace elements to such vines, perhaps once a month. This may be bought or, if difficult to obtain, made by yourself with 450g (1 lb) sulphate of iron, a pinch of copper sulphate (though this is best dissolved in water and sprayed very sparingly on the ground with a watering can kept for the purpose), 10g (½ oz) borax (boron) and 450g (1 lb) Epsom salts (magnesium). Add 2 teaspoons of this mixture to each 450g (1 lb) of balanced fertilizer.

A little hydrated lime applied in the winter months will condition the soil – even on chalky land – and do no harm. Sprinkle a small amount over the surface and allow winter rains to wash it in. Do not apply on a windy day.

In the open site of my Hampshire vineyard in southern England, I applied test strips across the rows of vines. Some were of lime, others trace elements, and more still of rotted manure from cows, chickens and pigs. Over several years of these experiments I could see no visible sign of difference in health, growth or fruit between control strips, with no treatment, and those under test. I concluded that the roots, said sometimes to descend 10m (30 ft) or more, took what they needed in nourishment and

Cutting bunches of grapes from the vine

Buckets of harvested grapes: Triomphe d'Alsace on left, Cascade on right

moisture on their way down, in this instance, through a thin layer of topsoil and thereafter solid chalk.

But in small gardens, especially where vines are in direct competition with other vegetation, watering and the application of some fertilizer and trace elements makes good sense.

SPRING AND SUMMER BLEEDING

Sometimes in springtime a vine will weep from a winter pruning cut. This may happen even before the buds swell or burst. The vigorous Baco No.1 is especially prone to bleeding. No harm will have been done. In fact, unless pools of (tasteless) sap appear as wet patches on paving stones below vines, you may be quite unaware of it happening. Cuts will heal in due course.

The same applies to summer pruning when excess growth is trimmed back for the sake of tidiness or to concentrate the vine's strength into forming fruit or growth.

TREATMENT OF BUNCHES ON THE VINE

For handsome bunches of table grapes, when vines like Black Hamburgh and the tender, though magnificent, Muscat of

Alexandria are grown in the greenhouse, it is advisable, though not necessary, to thin out grapes with pointed scissors to allow both bunches and fruit to develop handsomely. With hardy outside grapes like the ones with which we are concerned, grown mainly for decoration and wine, cosmetic care like this is quite unnecessary.

BIRDS AND WASPS

Birds may favour the grapes from some varieties of vine and ignore others. When there were few grapes on my London vines in their early years, the birds ate them all. When the fruit became plentiful, the grapes were ignored – until late in the season when surplus bunches were left on the vines for them as fattening food.

Netting a pergola, arch or arbour against the depredations of birds is an almost impossible task. With wall grown grapes it is much easier, when nets can be draped down and over the ripening fruit.

To defeat wasps in their insatiable quest for sucking dry such early ripening varieties as Siegerrebe, is very difficult. To hang traps made from jars or plastic bottles with a funnelled opening, baited with stale beer or diluted jam, may be of some help (the

Two ideas for wasp traps

65

top cut off a plastic bottle, reversed and inserted makes a simple trap). A better method in the countryside, but one needing patience and good eyesight, is to stand still at set intervals and watch for wasps departing from and returning to a nest (especially in the evening). Call in a professional Pest Controller or, if not in sympathy with those who consider insects to have rights, destroy them in their home yourself, with poison and fire.

NOBLE ROT, REDUCING LEAF COVER, SUMMER PRUNING

Noble rot

Although my recommended vine varieties are all disease resistant, in the latter part of the season some bunches may display signs of noble rot (the fungus *Botrytis*). This has the effect of shrivelling up some of the grapes in certain bunches. The mould that surrounds some or even all shrunken grapes in each bunch is brought about by humid weather conditions (though some vine-yard managers can now induce it with spray from aircraft). The result is a concentration of the grapes' sugar content. The greatest sweet wines are made with grapes infected thus. So add them to your vinification. If in doubt whether the rot is noble or not, test a few grapes on your tongue. Noble rotted grapes will be extra

66

sweet and very tasty, the taste of those rotted with grey mould will not be pleasant. If still in doubt, do not use them in your vinification.

As grapes begin to ripen it is beneficial to cut away some of the leaves that shield them from sunshine. This is particularly important in less sunny climates, when an abundance of leaves covering an arbour will prevent sun and air from reaching the fruit. To enjoy the sight of dappled sunlight shining through a thinned leaf canopy is in any case an autumn pleasure you should not deny yourself. The reduction of leaves will do no harm. Their contribution to the vine's health and growth will have been almost spent by late summer.

Never be afraid to chop off excess growth in summertime. The neatness of commercial vineyards is contrived by the use of mechanical hedge cutters.

HARVEST

By early to mid September (or later, depending on climate, altitude and variety), ripe bunches of grapes hang thick from the vines. It is time to have your vinification equipment ready (see page 71).

Let us first consider vinification. This may be accomplished, as so often in commerce, in a hygienic, stainless steel winery with chemists and their complex machinery monitoring each and every process. All is sterilized to the nth degree (perhaps even the chemists). At the other extreme, it may be done as it has been by peasants throughout history in the vine-growing world, by treading on ripe grapes, allowing the juice to ferment with the natural yeast on grapeskins, and swilling down the result.

The professionals err on the side of caution because huge sums of money are involved and errors are financially disastrous. Thus, chemical sprays (besides the usual ones of copper and sulphur), insecticides, additives, preservatives and all the rest are used. The resultant wine may be delicious, or it may give you a dreadful headache. Your own wine, being absolutely pure, will only give you a headache if you drink too much of it at one time.

From our small gardens we cannot, and do not, expect to make wine of the quality that comes from the great Bordeaux châteaux, especially from grape varieties that are free from mildew and rot. But what we are able to make is pure, fresh, rustic young wine that will be completely free of noxious additives and preservatives. Such wine is virtually unobtainable elsewhere. Moreover, with youthful wine in mind and expectations not of the highest, we are able to make it with the minimum of fuss and expensive equipment.

Even at the only time when any exactitude is called for (when determining the sugar content of the grape juice), guess-work can still take the place of precision. To measure or guess at this sweetness factor is to establish the amount of ordinary, plain, white domestic sugar that should be added to the grape juice to produce, after completion of fermentation, about 11 per cent of alcohol in the wine. Do not try to get much above 12 per cent.

As an indication, over the last few years when summer weather conditions have varied considerably, the blended juice from my grapes, when adding possibly a quarter of the less sweet Seyval Blanc, has in each year contained almost the same amount of sugar – 14 per cent, needing about 280g (10 oz) of sugar to be added to each gallon to reach 11 per cent in the wine. Red juice alone, mostly from Triomphe d'Alsace and Cascade, has contained around 17 per cent sugar, needing around 140g (5oz) per gallon.

Fermentation, from yeasts on the grape skins or from added yeasts, turns sugar into alcohol. Alcohol preserves the wine naturally and makes it a pleasure to drink.

A wine hydrometer to measure the relative density of the must (grape juice) and, with the aid of my chart (page 125), to tell you how much sugar should be added to the juice to reach the desired amount of alcohol in the wine, can be bought quite cheaply from a do-it-yourself winemaking equipment shop or drugstore. It will provide you with the exact information, using grape juice squeezed from a nylon straining bag or the first pure or blended juice to appear at the bottom of your fermentation bin at the start of harvest.

A %sugar refractometer, acquired at much greater expense, will do the same when used with the juice from any grape selected from your vine(s), and with blended or unblended juice. Refer to my chart to convert readings by various methods into the correct amount of sugar to be added to the grape juice to obtain the desired degree of alcohol.

A hydrometer could be the first item of your equipment to be purchased.

*Wine
hydrometer*

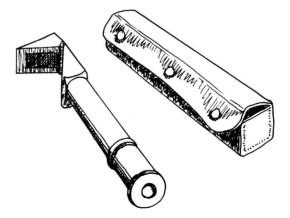

Wine refractometer

EQUIPMENT

For the winemaking process, you will need:

1. Wine hydrometer with thermometer, or refractometer (if not relying on guesswork) and my chart (page 125)

2. Yeast (wine yeast, or dried or fresh breadmaking yeast)

3. Sugar (domestic white)

4. Plastic bucket(s) (in which to harvest bunches of grapes, hold stripped stems and the skin/pip residue when straining juice into demijohns). Avoid any contact with metal throughout the entire vinification process

5. Lidded, plastic fermentation bin(s) of 15 litre/3 gallon capacity

6. A large plastic funnel

7. Nylon juice-straining bag(s)

8. A large kitchen bowl

9. 5 litre/1 gallon demijohn glass fermentation jar(s)

10. Bored out rubber bungs to fit them

11. Plastic, two-chambered fermentation locks to fit these bungs

12. 1.25m (54 ins) of 1cm (⅜ in.) diameter clear plastic syphoning tube, 33cm (12 ins) of 5mm (¼ in.) wooden

dowel rod and a cork to fit the demijohn; or a bought syphon

13. Wine bottles (6 per demijohn)

14. Bottle brush for cleaning bottles

15. A corking machine of some sort (and mallet or hammer if necessary). These come in many shapes, sizes and prices. Aim for the simplest, such as the one illustrated on page 85.

16. Corks – either new or top-quality used

You now have the equipment at hand and, happily, the cost of everything will have been small.

JUICE AND ITS PRESERVATION

Where to cut grape bunches when harvesting

Children will have eaten some of the ripe fruit, found that wine grapes are mostly pips, and clamour for juice to drink. Abstainers from alcohol may do the same.

Harvest some bunches of ripe grapes in your clean bucket, strip the fruit from the stems, put the grapes into a nylon straining bag, place the bag in a large basin or mixing bowl and, with the knuckles of your fists, force down on the bagged grapes, allowing the sticky juice to flow into the basin. Jug it. Continue extracting the juice by pressing, squeezing and twisting the bag. You have now made fresh, wonderful, rather viscous, pure grape juice.

If given access to warmth, the natural yeasts from the grape skins will very soon start a fermentation to turn the sweet juice into wine. So to prevent juice from fermenting, keep it cool in the refrigerator, or freeze it for longer preservation. Solids will settle. Decant off the clear juice if desired, or stir it up for a more full-bodied, though less attractive-looking, drink. If you would like to add sugar, and/or dilute the juice with water, do so. It will still be pure grape juice, unlike the commercial varieties that are treated by manufacturers for long shelf life.

The amount of juice obtained from a given quantity or weight of grapes will depend mainly on the size of the pips (wine grapes have large ones relative to the overall size of the grape) and thickness of the skins.

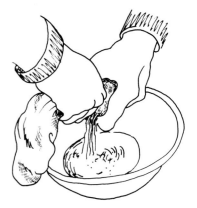

Squeezing juice from a nylon straining bag

WINEMAKING

The grapes are ready for their magical transformation into wine. A frost will not have harmed them.

Your equipment (see page 71) should be ready.

Test the grapes for sweetness by eating some. If they are sweet, strip some from their stalks into a fermentation bin to yield enough juice for a refractometer or wine hydrometer reading of a variety or blend. This reading, and reference to my chart, will tell you how much added sugar will be needed for each gallon of juice. A 15 litre/3 gallon fermentation bin of grapes will produce less than 15 litres/3 gallons of juice when the pips and skins have been eliminated (the volume depending on varieties used, skin thickness and juice yield for that season). Refer to the chart instructions. You are ready to continue.

Harvest the grapes into buckets, making a party of it if you wish. Or you may decide to work alone and unmolested.

From the brimming buckets you have harvested (and you will be surprised how productive grape vines are), hand strip more grapes from their stalks, putting them, whole, bruised or broken into the fermentation bin. Throw away the useless stalks.

There will be yeasts on the grape skins, but to add a wine (or breadmaking) yeast will help fermentation. The use of bakery yeast is frowned upon by purists (as is winemaking without sulphur), but it will help to start the fermentation quickly and thus build up an alcohol content to prevent noxious bacteria from entering and possibly spoiling your wine. However, it can impart its taste to the wine, especially at bottling time if the syphon is incorrectly adjusted. The total quantity of yeast to add to a 3 gallon/15 litre fermentation bin full of grapes would be, say, four packets of wine yeast (refer to the instructions on the container) or a tablespoon of dried or fresh bread yeast. I now favour mostly wine yeast with a little bread yeast.

Fill the bin, adding the determined amount of sugar and yeast bit by bit as you go, until it is all used. When your bin is as full as it could possibly be (unless it is a part bin at the end of the harvest), put on the lid, which has in it a small hole that will allow carbon dioxide to escape and, as it does, prevent noxious bacteria from entering. So make sure that the lid is firmly in place.

One person can harvest, de-stalk and fill a 15 litre/3 gallon fermentation bin in around three hours.

Do not expect instant fermentation. If the bin is kept in a warm spot (a warm kitchen is ideal), it will start to show in a day or two in the form of bubbling juice. However, even before this becomes apparent, it will be necessary (starting almost right away) to turn the grapes over with a clean wooden spoon. This task, which prevents unwanted moulds from forming on the surface of the skins, should be done two or three times a day. It will become much easier to accomplish as fermentation takes place in the juice and within the grape skins. When the 'cap' of skins and pips has been pushed down, more room in the bin will have been created, but adding extra grapes will cause spillage, and thus waste juice, besides making a dreadful mess.

Keep the inside and outside of the lid, the rim and sides of your fermentation bin immaculately clean. This will keep noxious bacteria at bay.

After a few days of fermentation and forcing down the floating cap and any parts of skins adhering to the sides, you will notice that, due to fermentation taking place within the grapes themselves and thus breaking down their structure, the pressure needed to push down the cap will have become very much easier. You will also notice that the fermenting juice, in the case of red wine, will have acquired a wonderful, deep ruby-purple colour. This emptying of skins and lightening of cap will probably have happened, depending on the surrounding temperature, in four to seven days. A week of fermentation in the bin will certainly be enough for adequate tastes and colour to be imparted to the wine from the grapes. The next process is at hand. As this is a messy one, it is best to work on a table covered with newspapers.

Place your large funnel in a demijohn and stretch the nylon strainer bag over it. Using a wooden ladle, almost fill the bag within the funnel with skins, pips and juice. Some strained juice

Fermentation bin, pressing down the cap

will now start to run into the demijohn. Squeeze more juice from the bag into the demijohn and then place the bag in the large kitchen basin. Press down on it with the knuckles of your clenched fists, then twist and squeeze the bag to extract the remaining grape juice from it. Throw away the spent pips and skins, return the empty bag to the funnel and add the juice in the basin to that already in the demijohn. (Do not compost the residue as the pips may produce many useless vines in the garden.) It will take from 1½ to 2 hours for one person to strain the contents of a 15 litre/3 gallon fermentation bin into demijohns.

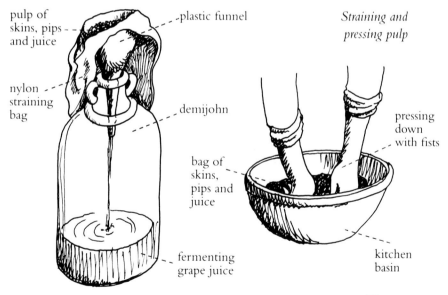

pulp of skins, pips and juice

plastic funnel

Straining and pressing pulp

nylon straining bag

demijohn

pressing down with fists

bag of skins, pips and juice

fermenting grape juice

kitchen basin

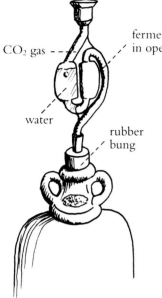

CO₂ gas ‑ ‑

fermentation lock
in operation

water

rubber
bung

*Demijohn and
fermentation lock*

Fill the demijohn to the brim in this way and insert the rubber bung containing a plastic fermentation lock that you have charged with a little water. Carbon dioxide gas is the product of yeasts turning sugar into alcohol. The fermentation lock will allow this gas to escape in the form of bubbles pushing out through the water chambers and will prevent noxious yeasts and bacteria from getting into the wine. The fermentation lock may at first fill up with lustily fermenting wine. Replace it with a clean one. Immediately wash out the gunge inside the chambers of the fouled fermentation lock with a vigorous flow of tap water.

Label the demijohns, noting vinification dates, the blend of grapes used, yeast, etc., and keep them in a warm place (such as a warm kitchen) to complete the fermentation. Use plenty of cold running water to wash and finally clean all your equipment.

Fermentation will continue in the demijohn until yeasts have turned all the sugar in the wine into alcohol. The wine will then be clear. The time taken for this to happen will depend mainly on temperature. Allow for a month or two. A layer of spent yeast will now lie beneath the wine. There will no longer be that satisfying sound of carbon dioxide bubbling forth. The fermentation locks will be idle, their water levels even, or nearly so. The wine will be dry and ready for bottling. Test some. (The settled yeast layer will not be disturbed if a straw is used for this.)

Do not leave your wine to lie for too long on the yeast layer after fermentation is complete, or the taste of yeast will be taken up by it. Bottle as soon as possible.

There is another 'fermentation', more prevalent in northern countries, when malic acid in the wine is turned into lactic acid. This may have followed directly after the yeast fermentation or could start in the spring or even later. It can be induced by professional winemakers or eliminated by sterile filtration or pasteurization. Should it take place in bottle, the result will be a slight prickle in the wine. No harm will have been done to it. But as we will bottle the demijohns for consumption as and when wanted, and soon, this 'fermentation' does not really concern us.

NOTE: As the air bubbling so satisfactorily from the fermentation locks is poisonous carbon dioxide, and builds up from ground level, it is not advisable to use an unventilated cellar for fermentation. In less sensitive times, the death of caged mice or canaries at ground level was a warning for those above to retreat.

BOTTLING AND CORKS

Buy a syphon, or make one that can be operated by one person. For this, use a cork suitable for a demijohn with a 1cm

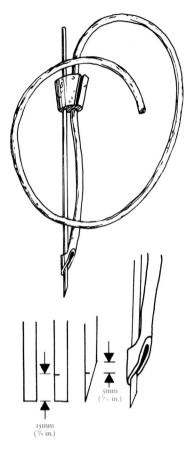

One-person operated
syphon

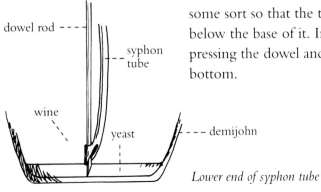

dowel rod - - - -

syphon
tube

wine

yeast

- - - demijohn

Lower end of syphon tube

Bottling and corks

(⅜ in.) hole bored in it for a fermentation lock. Drill another hole parallel to it for a 36mm (14 ins) length of 5mm (¼ in.) wooden dowel rod. With a sharp knife cut a small channel down the length of the cork to allow air to enter the demijohn as the wine is taken from it. Cut a sharp wedge at the base of the dowel and push the rod down through its hole in the cork so that with the cork in place, the dowel will touch the bottom of the inside of the demijohn.

Now, using a 1.25m (54 ins) length of 1cm (⅜ in.) diameter clear plastic syphon tube, push it down through the fermentation-lock hole in the cork. Cut a small slit across the bottom of the tube 15mm (⅝ in.) from its lower end. Starting from opposite this slit and 5mm (³⁄₁₆ in.) above it, slice diagonally to the end of the tube. Push the wedge end of the dowel into the slit and out of the end of the tube. There will now be an opening in the tube through which to syphon the wine (if not, pare away a litle more of the tube). Adjust the tube opening to take its wine from above the yeast layer when the dowel rod touches bottom.

Raise the full demijohn on to a tub, table or platform of some sort so that the tops of the bottles to be filled are well below the base of it. Insert the cork with its dowel and tube, pressing the dowel and tube down together until the dowel hits bottom.

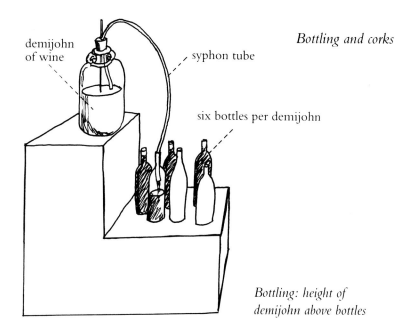

demijohn
of wine

syphon tube

six bottles per demijohn

*Bottling: height of
demijohn above bottles*

Using a bottle brush, wash your bottles in plenty of cold
running water. For one full demijohn of wine, have ready six
wine bottles (it will fill five and part of the sixth).

For each demijohn place six corks in a bowl. Pour boiling
water from a kettle over them and force them under the water
with a weighted saucer. Allow them to soak thus for ten minutes
and repeat the process. The corks will now have become sterilized, soft and ready for insertion with a corking machine.

Only because wine like ours is best consumed right away, or
within a few months of the vintage, is it permissible to insert high
quality used corks (their quality is often far better than those

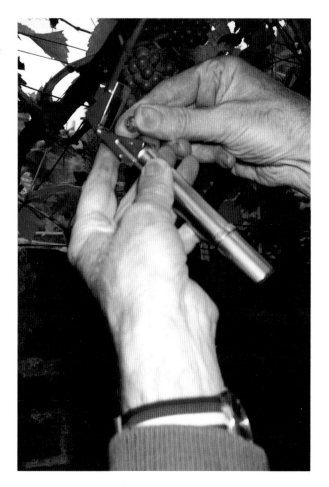

obtainable in the shops). However, for bottles to be laid down for experimental purposes, use new corks.

So now you have the demijohn standing well above the level of the tops of the clean bottles, the syphon rinsed and inserted, the corks soft in hot water, and a washed corking machine at the ready (with mallet or hammer at hand with which to strike the plunger). And because some wine will spill, make sure you have a mopping-up cloth handy or that the table, once again, is covered with layers of newspaper.

Hold the open end of the syphon tube below the base of your demijohn and suck on it with a long, smooth suck until the wine flows. (Several sucks, allowing the wine to return to the demijohn, will result in failure of the syphon and possibly wine clouded by yeast). Always keeping the end of the tube lower than the bottom of your demijohn, fill the bottles, allowing space in

To close the syphon tube, double it back on itself

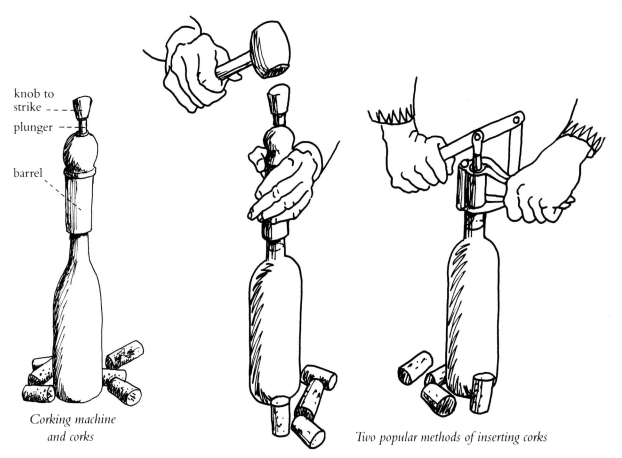

knob to
strike

plunger

barrel

*Corking machine
and corks*

Two popular methods of inserting corks

each for the length of cork. Between filling one bottle and the
next, you will need to close off the flow of wine by bending the
syphon tube back on itself (unless it is a bought one, in which
case it will have a tap). Even then a little wine is bound to spill.

   Cork your bottles, inserting the best end of the cork first.
Trim off any uninserted cork. You may want to consume the
wine in the partly filled bottle right away.

Stripping grapes from the stalks into the fermentation bin, with a spare bucket for the discarded stalks

Adding the determined amount of sugar and yeast as the fermentation bin is filled

Replace the lid when the fermentation bin is full

There may be a slight prickle in the wine that is rather pleasant. This could be due to a miniscule continuation of fermentation, perhaps malolactic (see earlier), or possibly derived from the natural properties of your soil (it often happens on chalky land). So keep the bottles standing upright for a day or two in case the corks ease out. If all is well, lay the bottles on their sides. There is no need to capsule your bottles; but there might be slight weeping if the corks are not tight enough.

After you have filled the bottles, there will still be a little wine lying above the yeast in the bottom of the demijohns. Decant it off the yeast into a glass or jug. Allow any yeast in this to settle, and drink the wine, or use it for cooking or the vinegar jar (see MOTHER OF VINEGAR, page 120).

Pour the spent yeast remaining in the demijohns over your compost heap (if you have one) and wash all the equipment in running water. When dry, store it for next year.

Colour-code your bottles according to their vintage with adhesive spots and/or label them with the year, blend, yeast, etc. After tasting the wine and judging its quality, make a note in your records of all relevant information and tasting notes.

NOTE: Bordeaux (claret) bottles are the best shape for stacking on each other. Wooden bins made of 20cm (8 ins) × 2cm (¾ in.)

prepared timber, with interior dimensions of about 50cm (19 ins) × 35cm (14 ins), will hold 30 bottles.

THE WINE

Your wine, red, white or rosé (the latter, in our case, being a blend of the juice from black and white grapes, unlike correctly made rosé where red grape skins impart a little colour to white juice before being extracted), will, if fermented out, be dry and contain enough alcohol for pleasure and preservation. It may be delicious, it may just be good, but it will most assuredly be fresh and pure. If it is of a rustic nature, powerful in taste and colour (as mine is), drink it not as an aperitif but with robust and spicy food. Then it will show at its best.

I believe strongly that home-made wine, using grapes grown in a small garden, should be drunk soon after it has been made. It will then be a special treat, as new wines seldom appear in the marketplace. Lay some down for the future by all means. A few years will be enough, as wine made from non-classic grapes will seldom, if ever, be great, however well it may have been made. Your laid down wine could be a great success; but your wine's main charm will lie in the freshness of youth.

Box bottle store

1. *Grapejuice fermenting vigorously in the bin. The 'cap' should be pressed down two or three times a day for up to one week*

1

3. *Ladle grapes and juice from fermentation bin into the funnel holding the straining bag*

3

2. *When the grapes have fermented they must be strained into demijohns. Have all your equipment ready before you start*

2

4. *Squeeze the bag into the funnel*

4

5,6. Place the bag in the kitchen bowl and knead it to extract more juice, squeeze the bag again and discard the spent pips and skins

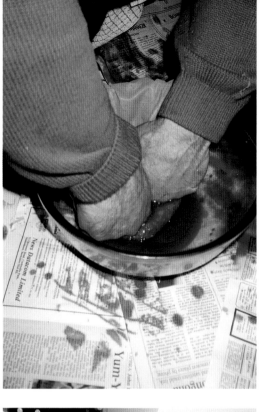

5

7,8. Replace the bag in the funnel and pour the juice from the bowl into the demijohn

7

6

8

The wine

Your wine will be different, distinctive – unique. Your methods, grapes, blends, soil, ways of cultivation, yeasts, wine-making skills, district, atmospheric conditions and much else will all go to form a wine unlike any other. And it will give boundless pleasure to both you and your friends.

Try making a fruit cup with either your home-made red or white wine. Using lemonade or soda water as the bulk of liquid, add ice cubes, wine, slices of apple, lemon or orange, a sprig of mint or borage, perhaps, and, to give it some 'bite', a little spirit of your choice – gin, whisky, brandy, ouzo, calvados, grappa, etc.

WINTER PRUNING AND CARE

It is December. The leaves on your vine, or vines, will have turned a beautiful colour, clothed your garden in a majestic cloak of red, yellow and gold, and then fallen. Gather them up for the compost heap.

Once the vines are naked of their leaves, it is time to prune them. If this is inconvenient in early December, it may be accomplished at any time during the dormant winter months, that is, until early March. But I believe it is better to prune early, for looks as much as anything.

summer growth

Two-budded spur of summer's growth remaining when winter pruned

For the vine framework, whether it be over an arbour or pergola, along walls or trelliswork, spur pruning is in order. All you need to know about this method is that grape bunches will form next year from buds growing from canes produced during the summer. So allow a cane with two buds to remain at each spur (branching point) and cut away all the rest.

Spur pruning

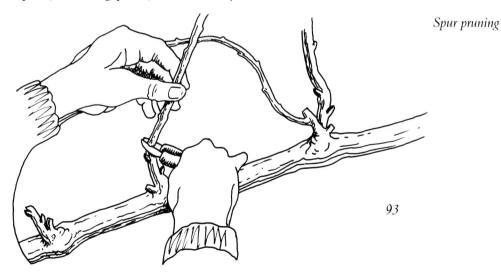

93

Spent skins and pips for disposal

Newly fermenting and week-old wine. Note fermentation reaching into fermentation lock, which will need changing

How to train a fountain-pruned vine

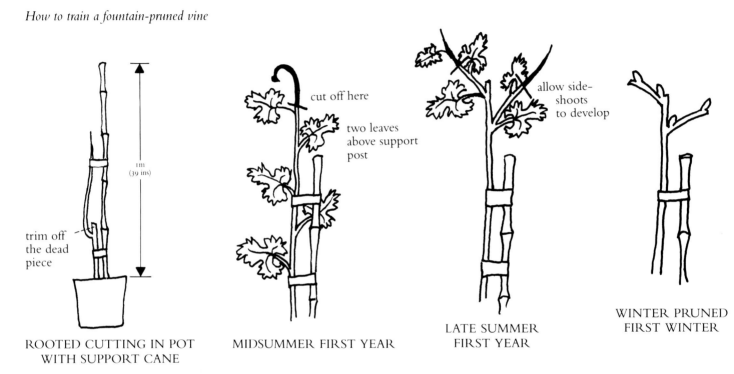

ROOTED CUTTING IN POT
WITH SUPPORT CANE

MIDSUMMER FIRST YEAR

LATE SUMMER
FIRST YEAR

WINTER PRUNED
FIRST WINTER

For a fountain-trained, free-standing vine, tied to a post in a pot, vegetable or flower bed, decide what height you wish the top of your 'fountain' of canes to develop. Stop off the vine immediately above a bud at the desired height. Retaining this bud and the one below it, rub off all buds that will appear thereafter lower down on the stock (trunk). New canes will form around

96

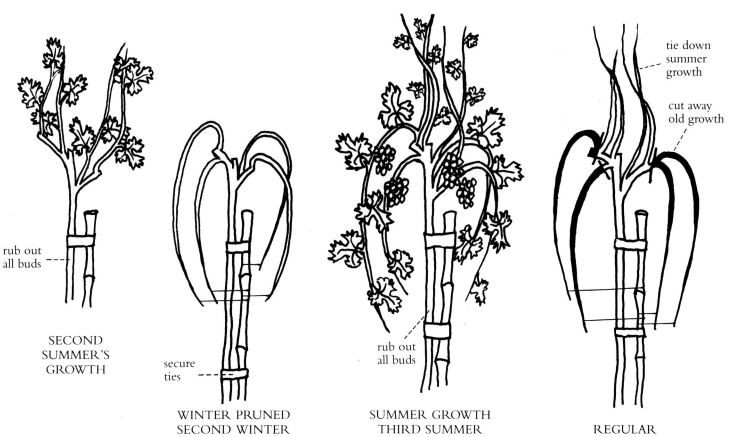

SECOND
SUMMER'S
GROWTH

rub out
all buds

WINTER PRUNED
SECOND WINTER

secure
ties

SUMMER GROWTH
THIRD SUMMER

rub out
all buds

REGULAR
WINTER PRUNING

tie down
summer
growth

cut away
old growth

the fountain point (spurs) in future years to be bent down and tied in to form the 'fountain'. At pruning time, when the fountain has become established, cut away the bent down canes that will have fruited, and bend down and tie in the new canes that will have grown upwards during the summer.

Bottling equipment prepared. Note bowl on left containing corks held down in hot water by a weighted saucer

Tasting the wine through a straw before bottling

ABOVE *Pushing dowel and syphon tube into neck of demijohn*

ABOVE RIGHT *Syphoning the wine into bottles*

RIGHT *Pouring off the remaining wine from the yeast in the demijohn after bottling. Allow the yeast to settle in the jug and then drink the wine.*

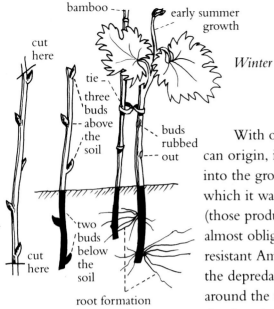

cut here

bamboo

early summer growth

tie

three buds above the soil

buds rubbed out

two buds below the soil

cut here

root formation

Cuttings

Winter pruning and care

With our mostly tough, phylloxera-resistant vines of American origin, it is perfectly all right to take cuttings to plant directly into the ground. The resulting vine will be identical to that from which it was taken (a clone). With the 'classic' vineyard grapes (those producing fine wines from *Vitis vinifera*), however, it is almost obligatory in Europe to graft cuttings on to disease-resistant American rootstocks. The vines will then be immune to the depredations of the dreaded phylloxera louse, a scourge that around the turn of the nineteenth to twentieth centuries developed a voracious appetite for vine roots, crossed national boundaries, and devastated most vineyards in Europe, causing much anguish and poverty. Many connoisseurs believe that the quality of wine made from grafted wines will never be as good as those made from the pre-phylloxera, ungrafted ones. Small outbreaks of phylloxera have reappeared in several places around the world; no-one knows quite why. Where vines are grown on sandy soil they seem to be free of this much dreaded creature.

A DIVERSIONARY NOTE ON PRUNING

If a vigorous vine, like Baco No.1, is left to run riot, every bud from every cane of the previous summer's growth will grow to become another cane and produce grapes, and so on and so on. The vine will then succesfully cover a large outbuilding and more with a complete and heavy tangle of matted wood, and grapes will form in summertime on the outer surface. But wherever vines are controlled by man and woman to produce grapes for the table, for juice or for wine, they must be winter pruned for ease of harvest and quality of fruit. Methods for this vary, but all rely on leaving some budded cane (or canes) from the previous summer's growth to form new wood and fruit. It is so with the spur pruning method described above, and with goblet pruning, a method more often used in hot climates, perhaps where more space is available, where stumpy, horn-like vines hug the ground; and in most vineyards, where two canes from the previous year's growth are tied down in opposite directions to low wires in long rows and the new growth is threaded up through a tramline of wires. This method, known as Double Guyot, could be used to advantage in a netted fruit cage, with rows of currants, gooseberries, raspberries and the like (see page 105). There are no rules. Amateur and professional alike, using pruners or hook-shaped knives, have their own ideas on how to prune vines for maximum fruit, quality grapes or decorative appearance. Methods, too, will depend on space and finance available as well as the prevailing climate, soil and site, not to mention time and labour cost. From a stretch of road running through the fertile plain of Catania, in Sicily, I saw vineyard vines

Mature vine,
goblet pruned

Prune vines with sharp
pruners of your choice

Put a softened cork into the corking machine

Place the corking machine on the bottle and strike the knob with a hammer

With the plunger completely down, the cork will be in place

The sixth bottle filled from a demijohn will be only partly full. It is time for a drink

trained in five different ways – in a fairly low canopy (probably for eating grapes); in Double Guyot form; with summer canes trained on wires in fan shape from a short trunk; in Geneva Double Curtain (along wires held high on rows of T-shaped posts); and in goblet form (page 101). But whatever method is used, the pruner (especially newcomers to the fun of it) must be decisive, severe and brave – for the sake of the vine's future and harvests to come.

TAKING CUTTINGS

From each year's prunings select your cuttings from healthy, straight lengths of ripened cane furnished with five buds. Either give these away for friends to plant and then enjoy the pleasures they offer, or put them into a cuttings bed with two buds below soil level and three above it, making sure that the buds point upwards. If the cutting is well watered, roots will become established throughout the summer months of growth, and the rooted cuttings can be transplanted or given away, clearly labelled, as presents in the dormant season.

Save some prunings to add a smoky flavour to barbecue cooking. Burn the rest and put the ashes on to the compost heap.

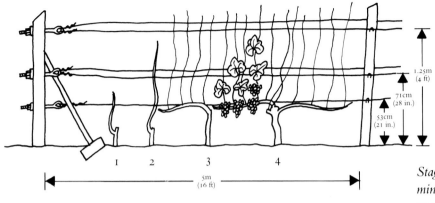

1.25m
(4 ft)

71cm
(28 in.)

53cm
(21 in.)

1   2   3   4

5m
(16 ft)

*Stages of progression for a
mini-vineyard when
pruning with the Double
Guyot method*

VINES IN A MINI-VINEYARD

The purpose of this book is to tell how simple, enjoyable
and productive it is to plant a vine or two in the garden, however
small, and reap the many benefits of husbandry, decoration, wine
and much else. But you may want to grow a few more vines and
create a small 'vineyard' – although I have never discovered how
many vines constitute a vineyard.

The ideal place for this is a netted fruit cage, growing in
lines with other soft fruit.

The most productive method of pruning, and the one that
takes up the least space, is the Double Guyot method. In a word,
the vines for this are planted in a row, or rows about 1.25m (4 ft)
apart – or a rotovator's width plus 30cm (1 ft) – with 1.25m (4 ft)
between vines. Support posts and wiring distances, etc., are
shown in the drawing (not to scale).

Leaves of Brant beginning to turn colour in the autumn. A few grapes are left for the birds.

Vine wood begins to ripen in the autumn

Dappled sunlight in late autumn

Geneva Double Curtain growing method

Vines in a mini-vineyard

The principle of pruning is simple enough. Having established a 'trunk' and a branching point, winter pruning simply involves bending down, in opposite directions, two canes from the previous summer's growth, tying them to a low wire so that their buds can grow upwards through supporting tramlines of wire in the growing season, and cutting away and discarding everything else that grew in the summer, except for a central bud or two to supply a choice of canes to bend down the following year.

The goblet method is used in hot climates, though I cannot see why it should not be used elsewhere, especially as no wiring or other additional expense is involved. New growth will certainly be more subject to wind damage unless tied together above, but with strict summer pruning by cutting away excess growth, this could be overcome. Against this method is the difficulty of cultivation around the spreading vines and the greater space demanded, for probably lesser crops than with Double Guyot.

Another method is the Geneva Double Curtain where the vines are trained along wires strung from the ends of cross-pieces along rows of wooden crosses. A disadvantage is wind damage to new growth and fruit, and, in a fruit cage, height. However, there is a bonus inasmuch as soft fruit such as strawberries can be grown beneath.

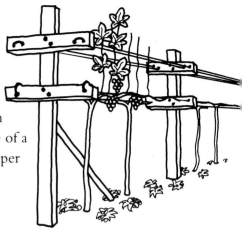

Although I have not seen it, the Geneva Double Curtain method could be developed by forming supports in the shape of a Cross of Lorraine and stringing tramlines of wire from the upper cross to support new season's growth.

KEEPING A RECORD

Cross of Lorraine growing method

Your year started with watching the buds on your vines burst forth with virginally green shoots. Bunches of flower buds appeared quickly after the unfolding leaves. Flowering and self-pollination took place, leaves grew larger, the vine spread and was controlled by you in the directions desired. Fruit formed and then ripened to be harvested. You vinified the wine initially by letting the whole grapes ferment in a bin and then strained the resultant juice into demijohns to continue its fermentation. The leaves turned colour and fell. The fermenting grape juice then finished its magical transformation into dry wine as yeasts turned sugars into alcohol and gave off carbon dioxide gas. With fermentation complete you bottled and corked the wine for drinking at your leisure. You then pruned the vines to give a winter aspect of order and tidiness. The vine and winemaking year was complete.

Spur pruning. Cut back to two buds

Spur pruning. Cut off all unwanted wood

Vine cuttings in a shady corner

If you are wise, you will make a record as you go along of this sequence of activities. It will form a pleasing, instructive and historical reminder of success and (may it never happen) failure. Record budding time, when flowering and pollination took place, fruit crop, harvest time, sugar content of grapes, the type of yeast chosen, the amount of sugar added, the duration of fermentation, vintage quantity and quality, colour coding or marking of bottles and the suitability and success of your vine varieties as providers of wine and/or garden decoration.

SUITABLE FOOD AND WAYS WITH WINE

You may have made full, dark, alcoholic, rustic wine (like mine) to be served at house temperature with powerful stews, game or cheese. You may have made a lighter, white wine, one ideal when cooled for drinks parties or for serving with meals of light food, such as chicken, fish or vegetables.

Your blend may have incorporated both red and white grapes and be of a rosy hue. Treat this in the same way as white wine, trying it both chilled and at house temperature. It, too, may be diluted and drunk as a fruit cup (see page 92).

The matching of wine with food is overdone, and only

really concerns those wanting to enhance a dinner party or who have an extensive cellar. Wine writers find it a useful theme to fill their columns. For most of us, any wine we like will go quite happily with any food we like. Reds with meat? Whites with fish? Perhaps as a general rule that is not a bad idea as red wines tend to bring out a metallic taste in oily fish. I found the reverse to be true with some wines made on the volcanic slopes of Mount Etna. The French, who know a thing or two about food and wine, are pleased to have red with fish, enjoying the extra fishiness that this can produce. There are no rules, other than the ones you may decide upon for yourself.

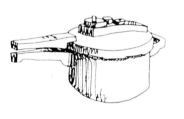

COOKING WITH WINE

Although wine is a splendid enricher of sauces, soups and stews, and a most important ingredient of many a marinade, if used too often it can become wearisome.

Two of the great French classic dishes involving red wine are Boeuf à la Bourguignonne and Coq au Vin. Here they are:

BOEUF A LA BOURGUIGNONNE

Pepper and salt a well-tied cut of beef of your choice. Whatever the size of the piece, always choose a lesser cut. Tender joints will tend to go stringy and dissolve. Put the beef into a fairly tight-fitting pot with a bouquet garni, a cut up onion, a little olive oil and a peeled garlic clove or two. Cover the beef with your very own red wine (even when it is still fermenting, if you like) and some gravy browning. Let it lie in this marinade for at least six hours (twelve to twenty-four will be better), turning it every so often.

Take the meat from the marinade and dry it. Pour the marinade into a jug or bowl. Rinse and dry the cooking pot. In dripping, lard or oil, brown the meat all over.

Now add the marinade to cover, and cook the meat very slowly on top of the stove or in the oven for three hours at least – longer if the piece is a large one.

An hour before you believe the meat to be ready, add to its cooking juices some very small onions, button mushrooms and pieces of smoked bacon.

When ready for the table, place the beef on its serving plate, discard the bouquet garni and thicken the juices in the pot with small lumps of butter into which you have worked some flour.

Allow this sumptuous gravy to cook for a little longer so that it thickens. Pour it over the meat, which should then be cut into generous slices. Serve with mashed potato and possibly another plain vegetable, like boiled carrots.

Instead of one piece of tied beef, some prefer to cook the meat in chunks. These are easier to serve but form a less spectacular presentation at the table. Meat cut into pieces will take less time to cook.

COQ AU VIN

First find your cock, as even meat from a large chicken will not provide the firmess of flesh required. Your best source for a good size cockerel is the Halal butcher, where you might have to order it. But in such an establishment they will gladly clean, skin and cut the bird into whatever size is required. You are now ready.

Marinate and cook the pieces in exactly the same way as for Boeuf à la Bourguignonne, though the cooking times will be slightly shorter.

Another excellent way to employ your red wine in the kitchen is by using it to marinate pork chops before cooking them. Here I give a recipe that I included in *The Oldie Cookbook* (Carbery Press, 1993):

TIPSY PIG

One of the great advantages of this simple recipe is that the pork chops gain a lovely colour and do not dry out when cooked. A son once complained at table that what he didn't like about Tipsy Pig was that he couldn't tell the difference between the lean (liked) and the fat (disliked), so much alike are they when cooked. However, you can trim off the excess fat anyway.

Take a shallow dish, the size depending on the number of chops (or other lean pieces of pork) required. Lay the chops on the bottom. Slice lots of peeled garlic cloves and place them around and over the chops. Add salt, pepper and a herb, such as thyme. Now almost cover the meat with your own red wine.

Do this in the morning for an evening meal, but turn the chops over a few times during the day. If you cannot manage this, completely cover the chops with wine when you are preparing the dish. But this will provide you with a little more liquid than necessary.

When ready to cook, pour off the wine and keep it aside. Dry the chops. Heat some olive oil in a frying pan and fry the chops slowly with the garlic. When cooked, lift out the meat and arrange on a warmed serving dish.

Pour the wine marinade into the frying pan with all the fried residues, brown garlic pieces and herb. Cook until it bubbles and reduces a little, while stirring it all around and scraping off bits that will have become attached to the frying pan. You will now have formed a brown and very tasty sauce with which to cover the chops.

Serve with mashed potato, rice, and/or a boiled or steamed vegetable.

One more splendid use for wine from your garden grapes is when making a natural gravy (rather like the one above).

After frying floured (and possibly spiced) pieces of chicken, veal or pork, place them on hot plates and add some wine to the drippings in the pan. Cook and stir for a short time and strain the succulent gravy over the meat before it is served.

SAILOR'S MUSSELS

This is an excellent recipe if you have made white wine and want to use some for cooking. Buy or gather an adequate quantity of similar sized mussels – say 1 pint or 500g (1 lb) for each person. If gathered from an unpolluted rocky shore, select un-encrusted ones that have been submerged by each tide. Let them spit out their sand for an hour or two in a bucket of clean, unsalted water. Then allow them to dry out in a colander.

Prepare mussels for the pot by placing them in a bowl of water under a running tap. Discard those that float or are heavy (probably full of sand or mud). If any are open, give them a good tap with the blunt side of a knife. If they close they are all right.

If they don't, discard them. Give the remainder a good scrub, scraping off any encrustations. Then place them in a bowl and cut off the beards with kitchen scissors or, using strong fingers or pliers, de-beard them by pulling out the filaments with which they were once attached to rocks or rope. Place them once more in the colander to drain. They are now ready to cook.

Put a glass or two of your white wine, a touch of vinegar and a mill or two of black pepper into a large saucepan that will allow plenty of space above the shellfish. Bring the wine to the boil. Add the mussels and, with the lid on the pan, give the contents a good shake up and around. Now bring the liquid to a foaming boil. Take the pan from the heat and shake them around again – top to bottom. Once more bring them to the bubbly boil. They should now be steamed open and ready.

Put the opened mussels, with their juices, into a large serving dish or into individual bowls. Sprinkle with chopped parsley and finely chopped onion. Each person extracts the meat from the opened shells by using a joined shell as pincers. French bread or, surprisingly perhaps, chips go well with them.

STUFFED VINE LEAVES

With no spray used, our vine leaves are quite safe to eat. Those from Baco No.1 early in the season are fine, as are Triomphe d'Alsace throughout the season and many others when young, large, thin and tender.

Cut the leaves from the vine and, pinching off the stem of each, put them in a large container and pour boiling water over them to cover. They will soon turn olive green, give off their distinctive smell, become soft and pliable and be ready to use when drained and dabbed free of water.

For the stuffing, boil rice (of any kind) for 12 minutes, drain it and place in a bowl with pepper and salt, chopped mint (fresh or dried) and pine nuts. Should the rice turn out to be glutinous, so much the better.

Lay each leaf, underside uppermost, on a flat surface. Firmly press some of the stuffing into a dessert spoon and place the lump of rice mixture somewhere near the middle of the leaf. Fold the leaf over the stuffing and continue to fold to make a parcel of it. Squeeze the parcel in the palms of your hands to extract any air and pack it tightly next to its fellows in a single layer in a shallow, ovenproof dish. When the dish is full, barely cover the leaves with stock, or stock and chopped tomatoes, or tomato juice. Sprinkle over some olive oil. Bake in a medium oven for up to half an hour, by which time the stock should have evaporated and the cooked vine leaves remain looking glossy and inviting in an oily coat. Eat them hot or allow to cool. They freeze well.

That is the simple recipe. But you may add all sorts of other things to the rice stuffing. Try cooked minced beef or lamb, fried onion and/or garlic, other spices, other herbs, other nuts (pounded) and whatever else you might feel to be good. But keep to a simple stuffing first, like the one I recommend.

Quantities will depend on the size of your operation, but half a pound of rice will go a long way. Any stuffing left over (and you will nearly always make too much) will make a fine rice salad when dressed with vinegar and olive oil.

MOTHER OF VINEGAR

Never throw away wine dregs in a glass, residues from vinification (free of yeast) or any that might have soured in the bottom of a forgotten bottle. Turn them into wonderful vinegar.

Buy a vinegar jar (*vinaigrier* in France), or two if you want to make both wine and cider vinegar. These are of glazed, brown stoneware, bulbous in shape, lidded, and with a wooden tap set in a corked collar about a third of the way up.

Pour in dry red, white or rosé wine (or a mixture), avoiding any commercial wine that has a strong smell of sulphur. Add enough adequately to cover the tap outlet. Replace the lid and wait, hopefully, until a mother has been created. Initially she will be thin, and look like an opaque disc of jelly – probably resting on top of the liquid, or just under it. This creation may take months. If you add a piece from an existing mother from another jar it will speed up the process no end. A good degree of surrounding warmth will also help. Don't be afraid to put your hand and arm inside the jar to feel if she has arrived.

With a mother *in situ*, she must be fed with wine or wine

dregs regularly. Try not to neglect her for more than two or three weeks at a time or she will starve. Wine tipped in to keep her upper surface moist is essential.

Once the vinegar has become strong enough (test some), you may draw it off when wanted, making sure that the contents of the jar are always above tap level.

Use this delicious, tangy vinegar with caution. It will usually be far stronger than that obtainable from the shops.

A wine vinegar mother will help to create cider vinegar – and vice versa. But cider and wine vinegar manufacture should be kept separate.

For pickling, cider vinegar is the cheaper to make (unless using your own wine). Almost fill the jar (they usually hold about 5 litres) and when the cider has reached the required vinegar strength, pour it into screw-top glass bottles. If you like, sterilize the vinegar (wine vinegar as well) by placing the uncapped bottles in a bain-marie for 20 minutes at 71 °C (160 °F). Screw on the bottle tops while hot.

Alcohol is necessary for the manufacture of vinegar, so non-alcoholic wine or American sweet cider will not do. Once the process in under way, ignore what goes on inside your jar (it is not a pleasant sight). Several mothers and children will form, any of which you may spare for a friend about to enter upon this delightful aspect of culinary husbandry.

After a year or so, delve in and discard any tired and ancient

lid

wooden tap

Earthenware 3-litre vinegar jar

mothers who will, by then, be taking up too much room at the bottom of the jar. They may even start to block the tap.

All this may sound a little 'earthy', but for most of the time you will just see a handsome jar in the kitchen, and be able to use the finest vinegar obtainable – almost for free. You will also have a good use for wine dregs after a party.

Your vinegar may lose condition at times (a state that I have never quite understood). Continue to feed the mother, and use the vinegar when it smells good after lifting the lid.

CONCLUSION

You have planted vines. You have enjoyed the growing of them, their shade, their colours, the fruit, juice and wine. You are immensely proud of your accomplishments. You have made many bottles of wine at almost no cost. You may have created vinegar as well. And all this stems from planting a vine or two in your small garden. Could you ask for greater reward?

HOW TO USE THE SUGAR/ALCOHOL
REGULATING CHART FOR VINIFICATION

The winemaking method described in this book is imprecise but very satisfactory and beautifully simple. Guesswork and ex-perience might do when calculating the amount of plain white sugar to add to grape juice to attain the desired amount of alco-hol in the finished wine, but the use of a wine hydrometer or a %sugar refractometer and the chart on page 125 is really advisable.

Fill your wine hydrometer with the first free-run juice in the fermentation bin from a variety or blend of grapes. Take the measurement. Find it in the left-hand column of the chart and go straight to the right-hand column to learn how much sugar per gallon to add to the grapes as you strip them from their stalks. The resultant wine will be over 11 per cent alcohol if you calculate that 15 litres (3 gallons) of grapes will make 15 litres of wine, which it won't (see overleaf).

If you would like a little more accuracy (I cannot see that there is such a need when making our kind of wine), take a reading as before and move to the instructions at the head of the second column (Oechsle). Take the temperature of the juice and subtract 1 Oe for every 20 °F below 60 °F and 2 Oe for impurities (though the latter subtraction relates more to when measuring

123

viscous juice from freshly *pressed* grapes). Having calculated the new Oe figure go to the right-hand column for the sugar quantities needed per gallon. Now comes more guesswork, because a 15 litre fermentation bin of grapes will produce less than 15 litres of juice (the volume of liquid depending on the bulk of pips and skins from the variety or varieties harvested, and the year). When you have made an estimate (say, subtract approximately 2 litres for 15 litres) and added the correct quantity of sugar, the resultant wine will be somewhere near 11 per cent alcohol.

For a refractometer reading, open the prism end of the instrument, put a drop of the initial free-run juice on the glass, close it and, focusing the instrument with the eye-piece, point it towards the light. The % sugar will be indicated clearly on the scale inside. Refer to column three and then the right-hand column.

A refractometer may also be used to gauge the sugar content of any grape as the ripening season advances.

NOTE

> 5 litres = 1 Imperial gallon (approx)
> = 1 ¼ US gallon (approx)
>
> 15 litres = 3 Imperial gallons (approx)
> = 4 US gallons (approx)

SUGAR/ALCOHOL REGULATING CHART
FOR VINIFICATION

WINE HYDROMETER READING AT 60°F Specific gravity of natural juice	OECHSLE at 60°F (pronounced Erksler) For each 20°F below 60°F subtract 1 Oechsle. For impurities subtract 2 Oe	REFRACTOMETER READING Sugar % approx. (Refractometers are an expensive luxury)	POTENTIAL ALCOHOL % (if the wine is fermented out without the addition of sugar)	Grams or ounces of sugar to add per gallon to reach the optimum of 82 Oe
1.085	85	20.1	11.2	
OPTIMUM				
1.082	82	19.4	11.0	0
1.080	80	18.9	10.6	2 oz (57g)
1.075	75	17.6	9.9	4 oz (114g)
1.070	70	16.3	9.2	6 oz (170g)
1.065	65	15.0	8.6	8 oz (228g)
1.060	60	13.7	7.8	10 oz (284g)
1.055	55	12.5	7.2	12 oz (340g)
1.050	50	11.2	6.5	14 oz (397g)
1.045	45	10.0	5.8	16 oz (454g)

ACKNOWLEDGEMENTS

All the photographs in this book were taken by the
author or Margreet Page-Roberts, with the exception
of those on pages 28 and 59 which are by Nigel Sutton.
The line drawings are by the author.

INDEX